BENNETT JAMES

Fit For The Top

How Fitness Shapes High Achievers

Copyright © 2024 by Bennett James

All rights reserved. No part of this publication may be reproduced, stored or transmitted in any form or by any means, electronic, mechanical, photocopying, recording, scanning, or otherwise without written permission from the publisher. It is illegal to copy this book, post it to a website, or distribute it by any other means without permission.

First edition

This book was professionally typeset on Reedsy.
Find out more at reedsy.com

Contents

Introduction: The Fitness-Success Connection	1
Chapter 1: The Foundation of Fitness	4
Chapter 2: Mental Toughness Through Physical Training	7
Chapter 3: Energy Management for Peak Performance	11
Chapter 4: Stress Management and Emotional Balance	15
Chapter 5: Building Confidence Through Fitness	19
Chapter 6: The Power of Routine and Consistency	23
Chapter 7: Nutrition: Fueling Your Success	28
Chapter 8: The Role of Rest and Recovery in Success	32
Chapter 9: The Mindset Shift: From Obstacles to...	37
Chapter 10: The Power of Community and Connection	41
Chapter 11: The Importance of Adaptability	46
Chapter 12: Fitness Success with Music (and How It Powers...	52
Conclusion: Fit for the Top	60
Appendix	63
Resources	68
Final Thoughts	71

Introduction: The Fitness-Success Connection

In today's fast-paced world, where the demands of career, family, and personal aspirations often seem to compete for our limited time and energy, the concept of success can feel elusive. Yet, amid the countless strategies and self-help philosophies available, one fundamental truth remains consistent: success is intimately connected to our physical well-being.

At first glance, fitness might seem disconnected from the traditional markers of success—money, power, status. But a closer examination reveals that the habits and mindset required to maintain physical fitness are the same qualities that propel people to the top of their fields. This book is founded on the idea that fitness is not just a component of success; it is a foundation.

Why is fitness so integral to achieving success? The answer lies in the holistic benefits that regular physical activity provides. When we engage in physical exercise, we do more than just strengthen our muscles or lose weight. We cultivate mental resilience, sharpen our focus, and enhance our emotional well-being. In short, fitness equips us with the tools needed to face the challenges of life head-on.

Consider the discipline required to adhere to a consistent workout regimen. This same discipline is necessary to meet deadlines, stay organized, and manage a team. The perseverance developed through physical training enables us to push through obstacles in our professional lives. Similarly, the energy boost provided by regular exercise enhances productivity, creativity, and the ability to think critically under pressure.

Furthermore, fitness contributes to emotional stability, helping us manage stress and maintain a positive outlook—both crucial for long-term success. The confidence gained from achieving physical milestones, whether it's running a marathon or simply sticking to a weekly exercise schedule, translates into a greater belief in our ability to conquer other areas of life. This is why so many of the world's most successful people, from CEOs to top-performing athletes, prioritize their physical health alongside their professional endeavours.

But the connection between fitness and success extends beyond individual achievement. In leadership, the physical presence and vitality that come from being fit can inspire and motivate others. A leader who embodies health and energy sets the tone for a productive, dynamic work environment. Additionally, the mental clarity and emotional balance fostered by regular exercise are invaluable in making sound decisions and leading with confidence.

In this book, we will explore how fitness can be your secret weapon in achieving and sustaining success. Through practical advice, real-life examples, and actionable strategies, you will learn how to integrate fitness into your life in a way that enhances your professional and personal achievements. Whether you're striving to climb the corporate ladder, launch a successful business, or simply lead a more fulfilling life, the principles outlined in this book will show you that being "fit for the top" is not just about physical health—it's about equipping yourself for lifelong success.

As we embark on this journey, remember, success is not a destination, but a continuous process of growth and improvement. And by making fitness a central part of that process, you can elevate not just your body, but your entire life.

Chapter 1: The Foundation of Fitness

When we think about success, we often picture the result: the big promotion, the thriving business, the recognition, or the financial freedom. But what about the journey that gets us there? The truth is success doesn't just happen—it's built on a foundation of habits, discipline, and consistent effort. And one of the most powerful tools for laying that foundation is fitness.

Now, when I say "fitness," I'm not just talking about hitting the gym or running marathons. Fitness is about much more than that. It's about building a strong, resilient body that can support a sharp, focused mind. It's about having the energy to tackle whatever life throws at you, and the discipline to stick with it even when the going gets tough. Simply put, fitness is about preparing yourself—physically, mentally, and emotionally—to succeed in every area of your life.

Let's start with the basics: Why does fitness matter so much? For one, our bodies and minds are deeply connected. When you take care of your body, you're also taking care of your brain. Regular exercise increases blood flow to the brain, which helps improve focus, memory, and mental clarity. It's no wonder that so many successful people swear by their morning workouts—they're not just getting in shape; they're getting their minds in the right place for the day ahead.

But it's not just about what happens in the brain. Fitness also builds resilience. Think about the last time you pushed yourself through a tough workout. Maybe it was the last few reps of a weightlifting session, or the final stretch of a long run. In those moments, your body wants to quit, but your mind pushes you to keep going. That's resilience in action. And the more you practice it in the gym, the more you'll find yourself applying it in other areas of your life—like when you're facing a tight deadline, navigating a difficult conversation, or working through a major project.

Another key aspect of fitness is discipline. Let's be honest: It's not always easy to drag yourself out of bed for a workout, especially when life gets busy. But that's where discipline comes in. By making fitness a non-negotiable part of your routine, you're training yourself to stick with something important, even when it's challenging. This discipline spills over into your work, your relationships, and your personal growth. It's the foundation of success because it teaches you to show up and put in the work, day after day, even when you don't feel like it.

And let's not forget about the energy factor. We all have the same 24 hours in a day, but some people seem to have endless energy to get things done. The secret? Fitness. When you're active, your body releases endorphins, which boost your mood and energy levels. You'll find that regular exercise doesn't just make you physically stronger—it gives you the stamina to power through your to-do list, tackle challenges with enthusiasm, and still have energy left over for the things (and people) you love.

So, where do you start? Building a strong foundation of fitness doesn't mean you need to become a gym rat or start training for an Ironman. It's about finding what works for you and sticking with it. Maybe it's a morning yoga routine to set the tone for the day, a brisk walk during your lunch break to clear your head, or a strength-training session a few times a week to build muscle and boost metabolism. The key is to choose activities you enjoy and that fit into your life.

It's also important to set goals—both short-term and long-term. These goals should be specific, measurable, and aligned with your overall vision of success. For example, instead of saying, "I want to get fit," try, "I want to run a 5 miles in three months," or "I want to be able to do 20 push-ups in a row." These tangible goals give you something to work toward and keep you motivated along the way.

As you begin to incorporate fitness into your daily routine, you'll start to notice changes—not just in your body, but in your mindset and your approach to life. You'll find yourself more focused, more resilient, and more disciplined. You'll have more energy to chase your dreams and more confidence to take on new challenges. And that's the real power of fitness: It doesn't just prepare you for success—it transforms you into the kind of person who can achieve it.

In the end, fitness is not just about looking good or feeling good. It's about building the foundation you need to succeed in everything you do. So, as you continue on your journey to the top, remember to make fitness a priority. Because when you're fit for the top, there's no limit to what you can achieve.

Chapter 2: Mental Toughness Through Physical Training

When we think of mental toughness, we often picture someone who can handle stress, stay calm under pressure, and keep going when the going gets tough. But here's a little secret: mental toughness isn't something you're just born with—it's something you can build. And one of the best ways to do that? Physical training.

Think about it. Every time you push yourself through a challenging workout, you're doing more than just strengthening your muscles—you're also strengthening your mind. You're training yourself to handle discomfort, to push past limits, and to stay focused on your goals, even when it's tough. This kind of mental toughness isn't just useful in the gym—it's a superpower in life.

Let's break it down. Imagine you're in the middle of a workout, and you're exhausted. Your muscles are burning, your heart is pounding, and everything in you is telling you to stop. But instead of giving in, you push through. You tell yourself, "Just one more rep," or "Just one more minute." And then, you do it. That's mental toughness in action.

Now, take that same mindset and apply it to your life outside the gym.

Maybe you're working on a big project at work, and you're up against a tight deadline. Or maybe you're dealing with a tough situation in your personal life. The ability to push through, to keep going when things get hard, is exactly what mental toughness is all about. And the more you practice it during your workouts, the more natural it becomes in other areas of your life.

But mental toughness isn't just about pushing through physical challenges. It's also about the discipline to stick with something, even when the excitement wears off. Think about those days when you don't feel like working out—when the couch looks way more appealing than the treadmill. Those are the moments when mental toughness really shows up. It's the voice in your head that says, "I made a commitment to myself, and I'm going to stick with it, no matter what." That kind of discipline is the backbone of success in any field.

Another aspect of mental toughness that physical training helps develop is resilience. Life is full of setbacks—missed opportunities, failures, unexpected obstacles. But just like in the gym, where you sometimes hit a plateau or have a bad workout, resilience is about bouncing back. It's about not letting one bad day (or even a series of them) derail you from your goals. When you're used to pushing through tough workouts, you develop a mindset that sees setbacks as temporary and surmountable.

Physical training also teaches you to stay focused. We live in a world full of distractions, and it's easy to get pulled in a million different directions. But when you're in the middle of a workout, you must be present. Whether you're focusing on your form during a lift, your breathing during a run, or your balance in a yoga pose, you're practicing the art of concentration. This ability to focus on the task at hand is a key component of mental toughness—and it's something that can

CHAPTER 2: MENTAL TOUGHNESS THROUGH PHYSICAL TRAINING

dramatically improve your performance in other areas, from work to relationships.

So how do you start building mental toughness through physical training? First, challenge yourself. It's easy to stay in your comfort zone, doing the same workouts over and over. But growth happens when you push yourself—whether that's lifting a little heavier, running a little farther, or trying something new that scares you a bit. Each time you challenge yourself and succeed, you're building mental toughness.

Second, be consistent. Mental toughness isn't built in a day—it's developed over time. The more you show up, day after day, the stronger your mind becomes. It's about creating habits that reinforce discipline and resilience, even on the days when you don't feel like it.

Finally, embrace the process. Building mental toughness isn't always easy, and it's not always fun. There will be days when you want to quit, when you don't see the progress you want, or when it feels like the effort isn't worth it. But these are the moments that define you. They're the times when you have the opportunity to dig deep, to prove to yourself that you're capable of more than you thought.

In the end, mental toughness is about developing the mindset that you can handle whatever comes your way. It's about building the resilience to bounce back from setbacks, the discipline to stick with your goals, and the focus to stay on track, no matter the distractions. And the best part? Every time you push yourself physically, you're not just getting stronger—you're becoming mentally tougher, too.

So, the next time you're in the middle of a tough workout, remember you're not just building muscles, you're building the mental toughness that will help you succeed in every area of your life. And that, my friend, is a skill worth every drop of sweat.

Chapter 3: Energy Management for Peak Performance

Let's talk about energy—because let's face it, without energy, even the best-laid plans can fall flat. You know those days when you wake up feeling like you could conquer the world, and then there are days when you're dragging yourself through the day, counting down the minutes until you can collapse on the couch? The difference between those days isn't just about how much sleep you got. It's about how you're managing your energy, and believe it or not, fitness plays a huge role in that.

When we think about success, we often think about time management—how to squeeze the most out of every hour. But time management alone won't get you far if you don't have the energy to back it up. That's where energy management comes in. It's not just about how much time you have; it's about how much energy you can bring to whatever you're doing.

So, how does fitness fit into all this? Well, the more active you are, the more energy you have—sounds counterintuitive, right? You'd think that working out would leave you more tired, but it's actually the opposite. Regular physical activity boosts your energy levels, keeps your mind sharp, and helps you stay focused throughout the day. It's like fuelling your body's engine so that it can run smoothly and efficiently.

Let's start with the basics: why does exercise boost energy? When you're active, your body releases endorphins—those feel-good hormones that give you a natural high. But that's not all. Exercise also improves your circulation, delivering more oxygen and nutrients to your muscles and organs. This helps your body work more efficiently, reducing feelings of fatigue and giving you that extra pep in your step.

But energy management isn't just about physical energy—it's about mental energy too. We've all experienced that 3 PM slump, where your brain feels foggy, and your motivation is nowhere to be found. Regular exercise helps combat that by improving your mental clarity and focus. When you're active, you're better able to concentrate, think creatively, and make decisions—essentially, you're bringing your A-game to whatever you're working on.

And here's the thing: you don't need to spend hours in the gym to reap these benefits. Even a short burst of physical activity can do wonders for your energy levels. A quick walk around the block, a few minutes of stretching, or a brief workout can give you the boost you need to power through the rest of your day.

Of course, it's not just about exercise. Nutrition plays a huge role in energy management too. Think of your body like a car—if you put in the right fuel, it runs smoothly. But if you put in the wrong fuel, or don't refuel at all, it sputters and slows down. The same goes for your body. Eating a balanced diet with the right mix of protein, carbs, and healthy fats keeps your energy levels stable throughout the day.

But what does "eating for energy" actually look like? It's about choosing foods that give you long-lasting energy, rather than those that cause a quick spike followed by a crash. For example, whole grains, lean proteins, and plenty of fruits and vegetables are all great choices. On the other hand, foods high in sugar or refined carbs might give you a quick burst of energy, but it's usually followed by a slump that leaves you feeling more tired than before.

Hydration is another key piece of the puzzle. Even mild dehydration can leave you feeling sluggish and tired. So, keep a water bottle handy and make sure you're drinking enough throughout the day. It's one of the simplest ways to keep your energy levels up.

Now, let's talk about balancing work, life, and fitness—because it's all connected. When you're managing your energy well, you're not just more productive at work; you're also more present and engaged in your personal life. You have the energy to spend quality time with loved ones, pursue hobbies, and enjoy your downtime. It's about creating a lifestyle that supports your success in all areas, not just in your career.

One of the best ways to manage your energy is to find a fitness routine that works for you—something that fits into your schedule and that you actually enjoy. Maybe it's a morning run that sets a positive tone for the day, a midday yoga session to re-energize, or an evening workout that helps you unwind. The key is consistency. When fitness becomes a regular part of your routine, it naturally boosts your energy levels and helps you perform at your best.

Finally, remember that energy management is a long game. It's not about going all out one day and crashing the next. It's about finding a sustainable routine that keeps you feeling energized day after day, week after week. It's about listening to your body, knowing when to push yourself and when to rest, and fuelling yourself with the right foods and habits.

In the end, managing your energy is one of the most powerful things you can do for your success. When you have the energy to give your best effort, day in and day out, you set yourself up for long-term success. And with fitness as a cornerstone of your energy management strategy, you'll find that you're not just surviving the day—you're thriving, with energy to spare for the things that matter most.

Chapter 4: Stress Management and Emotional Balance

L et's get real for a minute—life can be stressful. Whether it's the pressure of deadlines at work, juggling family responsibilities, or just dealing with the curveballs that life throws at you, stress is something we all must face. But here's the good news: how you manage that stress can make all the difference, not just in how you feel day-to-day, but in how successful you are in the long run. And guess what? Fitness is a game-changer when it comes to stress management and emotional balance.

First, let's talk about what stress actually is. At its core, stress is your body's response to a challenge or demand. It's that fight-or-flight reaction that kicks in when you're under pressure. In small doses, stress isn't necessarily a bad thing—it can actually motivate you to take action and get things done. But when stress becomes chronic, it can start to take a serious toll on your mental and physical health.

That's where fitness comes in. Regular physical activity is one of the most effective ways to combat stress. When you exercise, your body releases endorphins—those feel-good chemicals that help you relax and improve your mood. It's like a natural stress reliever that doesn't come in a pill bottle. And the best part? It's available to you anytime you need it.

But the benefits of exercise go beyond just those immediate post-workout endorphins. Over time, regular physical activity can actually help rewire your brain to better handle stress. When you're active, you're essentially training your brain to recover more quickly from stressful situations. You become more resilient, more adaptable, and better equipped to deal with whatever life throws your way.

Let's put it into perspective with a real-life scenario. Imagine you've had a rough day at work—your boss is piling on the tasks, a project isn't going as planned, and you're feeling overwhelmed. Instead of letting the stress build up, you lace up your sneakers and head out for a run. As you pound the pavement, you start to feel your tension melt away. By the time you're done, you're not just physically tired—you're mentally refreshed. That problem that seemed so big an hour ago? It doesn't feel quite as daunting anymore. That's the power of fitness in action.

But managing stress isn't just about blowing off steam. It's also about maintaining emotional balance. Life is full of ups and downs, and it's easy to get caught up in the highs and lows. Regular exercise helps smooth out those emotional swings. It keeps you grounded, helping you maintain a steady state of mind even when things get hectic.

One of the reasons exercise is so effective at maintaining emotional balance is because it helps regulate your body's stress hormones, like cortisol. When you're constantly stressed, your body is flooded with cortisol, which can lead to everything from weight gain to sleep problems to mood swings. But regular physical activity helps keep cortisol levels in check, which means you're less likely to experience those negative effects.

CHAPTER 4: STRESS MANAGEMENT AND EMOTIONAL BALANCE

Let's also talk about the mental clarity that comes with regular exercise. When you're stressed, it's easy to get caught in a cycle of overthinking and worrying. But physical activity forces you to be present. Whether you're lifting weights, doing yoga, or going for a swim, you're focused on the task at hand, not the million things on your to-do list. This break from your thoughts can give you the mental space you need to gain perspective and find solutions to whatever is stressing you out.

And let's not forget about the social aspect of fitness. Whether you're joining a group fitness class, playing a team sport, or just going for a walk with a friend, being active with others can be a great way to manage stress. Social support is a key component of emotional well-being and combining it with physical activity is a win-win. You're not just getting the benefits of exercise—you're also strengthening your connections with others, which can help you feel more supported and less stressed. And if you have that winning mentality, which is often needed in a career or business, achieving with a team is a great feeling.

So, how do you incorporate fitness into your stress management toolkit? It doesn't have to be complicated. The key is to find activities that you enjoy and that fit into your lifestyle. Maybe it's a daily walk, a weekly group fitness class, or calisthenics a few times a week. Whatever it is, make it a priority. Think of it as an investment in your mental and emotional health, just as much as it is in your physical health.

Also, don't underestimate the power of mindfulness in your workouts. Practices like yoga, tai chi, or even mindful running can help you stay connected to your body and breath, which is incredibly grounding when you're feeling stressed. These activities not only help you stay fit, but they also teach you techniques for managing stress and staying calm in the face of challenges.

In the end, managing stress and maintaining emotional balance isn't about avoiding challenges—it's about building the resilience to handle them with grace. And that's where fitness truly shines. By making physical activity a regular part of your life, you're not just strengthening your body—you're also fortifying your mind and emotions. You're giving yourself the tools you need to stay calm, focused, and balanced, no matter what life throws your way.

So the next time you're feeling stressed, remember: your workout isn't just about getting in shape. It's about taking care of your whole self—body, mind, and spirit. And that's a recipe for success that goes far beyond the gym.

Chapter 5: Building Confidence Through Fitness

Let's talk about confidence—because let's be real, confidence is one of those qualities that can make or break your journey to success. It's the difference between taking bold steps toward your goals and holding back because you're unsure of yourself. But here's the thing: confidence isn't just something you're born with. It's something you can build, just like a muscle. And one of the most effective ways to do that is through fitness.

When you think about fitness, you probably think about the physical benefits—getting stronger, losing weight, improving your health. But there's a huge mental and emotional component to it as well. Every time you push yourself through a tough workout, every time you hit a new personal best, you're not just transforming your body—you're transforming your mind. You're proving to yourself that you're capable of more than you thought. And that, my friend, is how confidence is built.

Let's start with the most obvious connection: how you feel about your body. When you're active and taking care of yourself, you naturally start to feel better about your physical appearance. It's not about fitting into a certain size or looking a certain way; it's about knowing that you're strong, healthy, and capable. When you feel good about your body, that confidence spills over into every other area of your life. You stand a little taller, speak a little more clearly, and take on challenges with a mindset that says, "I've got this."

But the connection between fitness and confidence goes deeper than just looks. It's about setting goals, working hard to achieve them, and then seeing the results. Think about the first time you accomplished something in the gym that you didn't think you could—maybe it was lifting a heavier weight, running a faster mile, or mastering a new yoga pose. That sense of achievement isn't just physical; it's mental. It's a reminder that you can do hard things, that you can push through discomfort and come out stronger on the other side.

And this confidence doesn't just stay in the gym. It follows you into the boardroom, the classroom, the living room—everywhere. When you've proven to yourself that you can overcome challenges in your fitness journey, you start to approach other areas of your life with that same mindset. You start to think, "If I can do that, what else am I capable of?" Suddenly, taking on a big project at work or speaking up in a meeting doesn't seem so daunting. After all, you've already proven that you're stronger than you think.

Another key aspect of confidence is resilience—the ability to bounce back from setbacks. And guess what? Fitness is an incredible teacher of resilience. Let's be honest: not every workout is going to be amazing. There will be days when you feel tired, when you don't hit your goals, or when you just don't have it in you. But every time you show up, even when it's hard, you're building resilience. You're learning that setbacks are temporary and that you have the power to keep moving forward, no matter what.

CHAPTER 5: BUILDING CONFIDENCE THROUGH FITNESS

This resilience builds an unshakable confidence. You start to believe in your ability to handle whatever life throws at you, because you've already handled it in the gym. That missed promotion, that tough conversation, that personal challenge—they're all just another set of hurdles, and you know how to jump them.

Let's also talk about the discipline that comes with a regular fitness routine. Discipline isn't just about sticking to a workout schedule; it's about proving to yourself that you can make a commitment and follow through. This self-trust is a critical component of confidence. When you know that you can count on yourself to do what needs to be done, you naturally start to feel more confident in your decisions and actions.

There's also something to be said for the mental clarity that comes from regular exercise. When your mind is clear and focused, it's easier to make decisions, solve problems, and stay on top of your game. This mental sharpness adds to your confidence because you're not second-guessing yourself. You're making decisions from a place of strength and certainty.

And once again, let's not forget about the social aspect of fitness. Whether you are part of a gym, a running group, or an online fitness community, being around others who are working toward similar goals can be incredibly empowering. It's motivating to see others push themselves, and it's even more powerful to be part of a community that supports and encourages you. This social support can do wonders for your confidence, reminding you that you're not alone on this journey.

So how do you build confidence through fitness? Start by setting small, achievable goals that challenge you but are within reach. What gets measured, gets done! Consider keeping a plan of your goals, tracking the performance in a diary, notebook or on your phone. Each time you hit a goal, celebrate it—it's a step toward building your confidence. Then, gradually push yourself to do more. Try new activities, increase the intensity of your workouts, and step out of your comfort zone. The more you challenge yourself, the more opportunities you have to prove to yourself just how capable you are.

Remember, building confidence is a journey, not a destination. It's something you cultivate over time, through consistent effort and a willingness to push yourself. And fitness is one of the most powerful tools you have in that process. By taking care of your body, challenging your limits, and sticking with your goals, you're not just building muscle—you're building the kind of confidence that can take you anywhere you want to go.

So the next time you're lacing up your sneakers or unrolling your yoga mat, remember: you're not just working out—you're building the foundation for a more confident, successful life. And that's something to be proud of, every single day.

Chapter 6: The Power of Routine and Consistency

Let's dive into something that might not sound as exciting as a new workout routine or a fitness gadget, but is absolutely crucial for success in fitness—and in life: routine and consistency. Yeah, I know, the words "routine" and "consistency" might make you think of boring, monotonous days where every hour is planned out to the minute. But stick with me, because when it comes to reaching your goals, these two words are pure gold.

First off, let's get one thing straight: consistency isn't about being perfect. It's not about never missing a workout or always eating perfectly. It's about showing up, day after day, even when you don't feel like it. It's about creating habits that move you closer to your goals, one step at a time. And the more consistent you are, the more those small steps start to add up to big results.

Think of it like this: success, whether in fitness or any other area of life, is rarely about doing something extraordinary once. It's about doing the ordinary things, consistently, over time. It's like the difference between saving a small amount of money every month versus trying to get rich with one big gamble. The consistent saver will almost always come out ahead. The same goes for fitness. You don't need to go all out every single day—you just need to keep showing up.

Let's break it down with an example. Say you've set a goal to run a 5 miles. On day one, you might struggle to run even a mile without stopping. But if you stick with it, running three or four times a week, gradually increasing your distance, guess what happens? By the end of a few months, that 5 miles seems totally doable. It's not because you made a huge leap all at once—it's because you kept at it, week after week. That's the power of consistency.

Now, let's talk about routine. If consistency is the "what," routine is the "how." Routine is the structure you put in place to make sure you stay consistent. It's about creating a daily or weekly schedule that supports your goals, so you're not constantly relying on motivation or willpower to get things done. Because let's be honest, there will be days when motivation is nowhere to be found. That's where a solid routine comes in.

The beauty of a routine is that it takes the guesswork out of your day. When you have a set time for your workout, a plan for your meals, and a schedule for your tasks, you don't have to waste mental energy deciding what to do next. You just follow the plan. This frees up your brain to focus on other things—like crushing your goals.

But here's the thing: your routine doesn't have to be rigid or boring. It should be something that fits your lifestyle and that you actually enjoy. If you're not a morning person, don't force yourself to work out at 5 AM. Find a time that works for you, and stick with it. The key is to make your routine sustainable, so it becomes a natural part of your day, rather than something you have to force yourself to do.

CHAPTER 6: THE POWER OF ROUTINE AND CONSISTENCY

Let's get practical. How do you build a routine that supports your goals? Start by identifying your priorities. What are the things that are most important to you, the things that will move you closer to your goals? Maybe it's getting in a workout every day, eating a healthy breakfast, or setting aside time for relaxation. Whatever it is, make those things non-negotiable. They become the anchors of your routine.

Next, map out your day or week. Look at your schedule and figure out where those priority activities fit in. Maybe it's a morning workout, a healthy lunch prep session on Sundays, or a nightly wind-down routine to help you sleep better. The goal is to create a routine that's flexible enough to adapt to life's ups and downs, but structured enough to keep you on track.

And don't forget to include some time for rest and recovery in your routine. This is where a lot of people trip up—they go all-in for a few weeks, burn themselves out, and then crash. But consistency isn't just about working hard; it's also about working smart. Rest days, recovery workouts, and downtime are all essential parts of a routine that will keep you going for the long haul.

One of the best things about having a routine is that it builds momentum. The more you stick with it, the easier it becomes. You start to see progress, which motivates you to keep going. It's like a positive feedback loop: consistency builds results, results build confidence, and confidence fuels more consistency.

But what happens when life throws you a curveball—when your routine gets disrupted by a busy work week, a vacation, or just the unexpected stuff that happens? This is where flexibility comes in. Being consistent doesn't mean being rigid. It means being adaptable. Maybe you can't make it to the gym, but you can do a quick workout at home. A quick 10–15-minute sequence of push ups, sit ups, squats, running on the spot can do wonders for adaptability. Maybe you're traveling and can't stick to your usual meal plan, but you can make the best choices available. The key is to stay focused on your goals, even if you have to adjust the plan.

In the end, routine and consistency are about making your success inevitable. When you have a routine that supports your goals and you stick with it consistently, you're setting yourself up for success. You're creating habits that make it easier to do the things you need to do, even on the days when you don't feel like it.

So, if you're looking for a secret to long-term success in fitness (and in life), this is it: show up, consistently, and stick to a routine that works for you. It might not sound flashy, but it's incredibly powerful. Over time, those small, consistent actions add up to big results. And before you know it, you'll be looking back, amazed at how far you've come—one routine day at a time.

THANK YOU!

Let me pause the learning for now to warmly thank you for joining me on this journey through fitness and success. Your experience and feedback are incredibly valuable, not just to me, but to others who may be considering this book to help guide their own paths.

If you've found the insights, tips, and options in this book helpful, I would greatly appreciate it if you could take a few moments to leave an honest review and rating. Whether you picked up this book online, in a bookstore, or through a friend, your thoughts can make a big difference.

Your review helps other readers discover the book and decide if it's the right fit for them. More importantly, it's a way for us to continue the conversation about fitness, success, and the power of making positive changes in our lives.

Thank you for your support, and here's to your continued success on this journey!

Keep reading, learning and applying, so you can be "**Fit for the Top**". *Fit for your top!*

Chapter 7: Nutrition: Fueling Your Success

Alright, let's get into a topic that's as crucial as it is sometimes confusing, that topic is nutrition. Now, if you've spent any time scrolling through fitness or health blogs, you've probably been bombarded with all sorts of conflicting advice about what to eat, when to eat, and how much to eat. It can feel like you need a degree in nutrition just to figure out what to have for lunch. But here's the truth: while there's a lot of science behind it, nutrition doesn't have to be complicated. In fact, the basics are straightforward, and when you get them right, you'll be amazed at how much better you feel, both in your fitness journey and in your daily life.

Let's start with the idea that food is fuel. This might sound like a cliché, but it's true. Your body is an incredibly complex machine, and just like any machine, it needs the right fuel to run efficiently. The food you eat provides the energy your body needs to move, think, and perform at its best. But it's not just about calories—what you eat matters just as much as how much you eat.

Think of your body like a high-performance car. You wouldn't fill it up with low-grade fuel and expect it to run smoothly, right? The same goes for your body. If you're constantly feeding it junk food, processed snacks, and sugary drinks, you're not giving it the high-quality fuel it needs to function properly. Sure, you might get by for a while, but over time, you'll start to feel sluggish, tired, and less focused. On the other hand, when you fuel your body with nutritious, whole foods, you're giving it the tools it needs to perform at its best—both in and out of the gym.

So, what does good nutrition look like? It's not about following the latest fad diet or cutting out entire food groups. It's about balance and variety. Your body needs a mix of macronutrients—carbohydrates, proteins, and fats—as well as a range of vitamins and minerals to function optimally. Let's break it down a bit:

Carbohydrates: Carbs are your body's main source of energy, especially during exercise. But not all carbs are created equal. Simple carbs, like sugar and white bread, can give you a quick burst of energy, but they're quickly digested and can lead to energy crashes. Complex carbs, like whole grains, fruits, and vegetables, are digested more slowly, providing a steady supply of energy. If you want to fuel your workouts and stay energized throughout the day, focus on complex carbs.

Proteins: Protein is essential for building and repairing muscles, which makes it especially important if you're working out regularly. But protein isn't just for bodybuilders—it's also crucial for maintaining your overall health, supporting your immune system, and keeping you feeling full and satisfied. Good sources of protein include lean meats, fish, eggs, dairy, beans, and nuts.

Fats: Fats often get a bad rap, but they're actually an important part of a healthy diet. They help your body absorb vitamins, provide long-lasting energy, and keep your skin and hair healthy. The key is to focus on healthy fats, like those found in avocados, nuts, seeds, and olive oil, while limiting unhealthy fats, like those in fried foods and baked goods.

Vitamins and Minerals: These micro nutrients might be needed in smaller amounts than carbs, proteins, and fats, but they're just as important. They play a role in everything from bone health to immune function to energy production. The best way to get a wide range of vitamins and minerals is to eat a colorful, varied diet that includes plenty of fruits and vegetables.

Now, I know what you're thinking—this all sounds great, but how do you put it into practice? The good news is that eating a balanced, nutritious diet doesn't have to be complicated or time-consuming. Here are a few simple tips to help you get started:

Plan your meals: One of the easiest ways to stay on track with your nutrition is to plan your meals ahead of time. This doesn't mean you have to prep every single meal for the week on Sunday (unless that's your thing), but having a general idea of what you're going to eat each day can help you avoid the temptation of grabbing fast food or processed snacks when you're hungry and in a hurry.

Make it easy: Keep healthy snacks on hand, like fruits, nuts, or yogurt, so you're not tempted to reach for chips or cookies when hunger strikes. And don't be afraid to take shortcuts, like using prewashed salad greens or frozen veggies—they're just as nutritious as fresh, and they can save you a ton of time.

Listen to your body: Your body is pretty good at telling you what it needs, if you pay attention. If you're feeling sluggish, it might be a sign that you need more carbs or water. If you're constantly hungry, you might need more protein or healthy fats. Learn to tune into your hunger and fullness cues, and adjust your eating habits accordingly.

CHAPTER 7: NUTRITION: FUELING YOUR SUCCESS

Don't stress about perfection: Nobody eats perfectly all the time, and that's okay. The goal is to make more good choices than bad ones, and to build healthy habits that you can stick with for the long term. If you slip up and have a slice of cake or a bag of chips, don't beat yourself up—just get back on track with your next meal.

It's also worth mentioning that nutrition is deeply personal. What works for one person might not work for another, so it's important to find a way of eating that makes you feel good and supports your goals. If you're not sure where to start, consider talking to a registered dietitian or nutritionist who can help you create a personalized plan.

At the end of the day, good nutrition is about more than just fueling your workouts—it's about fuelling your life. When you eat well, you feel better, sleep better, think clearer, and have more energy to pursue your passions and achieve your goals. It's one of the most powerful tools you have in your journey to success, so don't underestimate it.

So, next time you're filling your plate, remember that you're not just eating to satisfy your hunger—you're eating to fuel your success. Make it count!

Chapter 8: The Role of Rest and Recovery in Success

Let's talk about something that doesn't get nearly enough credit in the world of fitness and success—rest and recovery. We live in a culture that glorifies the hustle, where "grinding" and "no days off" are worn like badges of honor. But here's the thing: if you're constantly running on empty, eventually, you're going to crash. Rest and recovery aren't just nice-to-haves—they're essential parts of the equation for long-term success, both in your fitness journey and in life.

First off, let's clear up a common misconception: rest isn't the enemy of progress. In fact, it's the opposite. When you're working out, you're actually breaking down your muscles. It's during rest and recovery that those muscles repair and grow stronger. If you skip this crucial phase, you're not giving your body the chance to rebuild itself, which can lead to burnout, injury, and stalled progress. So, if you want to get stronger, faster, or fitter, rest isn't optional—it's mandatory.

But recovery isn't just about taking a day off from the gym. It's a holistic process that involves more than just giving your muscles a break. It's about recharging your entire system—body, mind, and soul. Let's break it down a bit.

CHAPTER 8: THE ROLE OF REST AND RECOVERY IN SUCCESS

1. Physical Recovery: Letting Your Body Heal

Physical recovery is probably what comes to mind first when you think about rest. This includes everything from getting enough sleep to giving your muscles time to repair after a workout. Sleep, in particular, is a game-changer. During sleep, your body goes into repair mode, releasing growth hormones that help your muscles recover and grow. If you're skimping on sleep, you're not just going to feel tired—you're also short-changing your body's ability to bounce back from tough workouts.

But sleep isn't the only aspect of physical recovery. There's also active recovery, which involves low-intensity activities that help keep your blood flowing and muscles loose without putting too much strain on your body. Think yoga, walking, or light stretching. These activities help reduce muscle soreness, improve flexibility, and keep you feeling fresh for your next workout.

Hydration and nutrition play crucial roles here too. After a workout, your muscles are like sponges, ready to soak up the nutrients they need to repair and rebuild. That's why it's important to refuel with a good mix of protein and carbs after exercising. And staying hydrated? That's non-negotiable. Water helps flush out toxins, delivers nutrients to your cells, and keeps your joints lubricated. So, drink up!

2. Mental Recovery: Recharging Your Mind

Now, let's talk about mental recovery, which is just as important as physical recovery. In our go-go-go culture, it's easy to underestimate the toll that constant stress, decision-making, and multitasking can take on your mental health. Just like your muscles need time to repair, your brain needs downtime to process, reset, and recharge.

Mental recovery can take many forms. It might mean stepping away from work to spend time with loved ones, indulging in a hobby, a movie, reading a good book like you are now or simply doing nothing for a while. Yep, you heard that right—sometimes the best thing you can do for your mental health is to just be. No goals, no to-do lists, no pressure. Giving your brain a break helps prevent burnout, boosts creativity, and improves your focus when it's time to get back to work.

Meditation is another powerful tool for mental recovery. Even just a few minutes a day can help reduce stress, improve concentration, and promote a sense of calm. If meditation isn't your thing, consider other mindfulness practices like deep breathing exercises, journaling, or spending time in nature. The goal is to create space for your mind to unwind and rejuvenate.

3. Emotional and Spiritual Recovery: Connecting with Yourself

Finally, let's touch on emotional and spiritual recovery. This is about taking care of your inner self, the part of you that needs connection, purpose, and peace. When we're caught up in the hustle, it's easy to lose sight of the things that truly matter—our values, our passions, our relationships. Emotional recovery is about reconnecting with these core aspects of who you are.

This might mean spending time with loved ones, practicing gratitude, or engaging in activities that bring you joy and fulfillment. It could also involve reflecting on your goals and the bigger picture of your life. Are you living in alignment with your values? Are you pursuing what truly matters to you? Taking time to answer these questions can help you stay grounded and focused on what's really important.

Spiritual recovery doesn't necessarily mean religious practices (though it can, if that's meaningful to you). It's more about finding a sense of peace and connection—whether that's through prayer, meditation, time in nature, or simply being still and present. This kind of recovery helps you stay centered and resilient, even when life gets chaotic.

4. Building Rest and Recovery into Your Routine

So, how do you make sure rest and recovery are part of your routine? It starts with a mindset shift—recognizing that rest isn't a luxury or a sign of weakness. It's a critical component of success. Once you embrace that, it's easier to prioritize it in your daily life.

Start by scheduling rest days into your workout routine. These aren't "cheat days" or days when you're being lazy—they're essential for your body's growth and progress. On rest days, focus on activities that help you recover, like stretching, foam rolling, or taking a leisurely walk.

Make sleep a priority, too. This might mean setting a consistent bedtime, creating a calming evening routine, or making your bedroom a restful sanctuary. Remember, quality sleep is one of the most powerful tools you have for recovery.

For mental and emotional recovery, carve out time in your week for activities that recharge you. This could be as simple as reading a book, spending time in nature, or enjoying a hobby you love. And don't forget to take regular breaks throughout your day to step away from work, clear your mind, and reset your focus.

Finally, check in with yourself regularly. How are you feeling—physically, mentally, emotionally? If you're feeling drained or burnt out, it might be a sign that you need to dial up your recovery efforts. Listen to your body and your mind—they're pretty good at telling you what they need.

In the end, rest and recovery are about giving yourself the space and time to grow, heal, and thrive. They're not just the antidote to burnout—they're the secret sauce that makes sustained success possible. So, the next time you're tempted to push through exhaustion or skip a rest day, remember that rest is where the magic happens. Embrace it, and watch your progress soar.

Chapter 9: The Mindset Shift: From Obstacles to Opportunities

Let's get real about something that everyone faces on the road to success: obstacles. Whether you're working toward fitness goals, career milestones, or personal achievements, there will be bumps in the road. But here's the thing—how you view and respond to those obstacles can make all the difference. It's all about mindset. In this chapter, we're going to dive into the power of shifting your mindset from seeing obstacles as roadblocks to viewing them as opportunities for growth and learning.

Embracing the Growth Mindset

You've probably heard about the "growth mindset" before, but let's break it down. A growth mindset is the belief that your abilities, intelligence, and talents can be developed through hard work, dedication, and learning. It's the opposite of a "fixed mindset," which is the belief that your qualities are set in stone and that failure is a sign that you're not good enough.

When you have a growth mindset, obstacles become opportunities to improve. Instead of thinking, "I can't do this," you start thinking, "I can't do this yet." That little word, "yet," is powerful. It shifts your perspective from a place of limitation to a place of potential.

For example, let's say you're trying to run a marathon, but you're struggling to increase your distance. A fixed mindset might tell you, "I'm just not a runner," and lead you to give up. But with a growth mindset, you'd recognize that every struggle is part of the process. You might think, "This is tough, but it's making me stronger. I'll keep working at it." With this mindset, you're more likely to stick with your training, learn from your setbacks, and eventually cross that finish line.

Reframing Failures

We've all been there: you set a goal, work hard, and then something goes wrong. Maybe you miss a deadline, fail a test, or fall short in a competition. It's easy to see these moments as failures, but what if you reframed them as valuable learning experiences instead?

Failure is one of the best teachers you'll ever have—if you're willing to learn from it. Every time something doesn't go according to plan, you have a choice: you can either let it define you, or you can use it as fuel to come back stronger. Instead of beating yourself up over a setback, ask yourself, "What can I learn from this?" Maybe you need to tweak your approach, develop a new skill, or simply be more patient with yourself. Whatever the lesson, embrace it.

Remember, everyone who's ever achieved something great has failed along the way. The difference is that they didn't let failure stop them. They used it as a stepping stone to get better. So the next time you face a setback, don't see it as the end of the road—see it as a curve that's helping you navigate to your ultimate destination.

The Power of Perseverance

Perseverance is the secret sauce of success. It's what keeps you going when things get tough. But here's the thing: perseverance isn't just about grinding it out through hard times. It's also about having the patience and determination to keep going, even when progress feels slow.

Think about it like this: imagine you're climbing a mountain. The top represents your goal, and every step you take brings you closer to it. Some days, you'll make big strides and feel like you're soaring up the slope. Other days, you might barely make it a few feet. The key is to keep moving forward, no matter how small the steps might be.

Perseverance is also about staying committed to your goals, even when the initial excitement wears off. At the start of any journey, it's easy to be motivated and enthusiastic. But as time goes on, that motivation can fade. Perseverance is what helps you push through those moments of doubt, boredom, or frustration. It's the belief that every step forward, no matter how small, is bringing you closer to success.

Shifting Your Perspective

One of the most powerful things you can do when faced with an obstacle is to shift your perspective. Instead of focusing on what's going wrong, focus on what's within your control. What can you do to move forward? What opportunities does this challenge present?

For example, let's say you've hit a plateau in your fitness journey. Instead of getting frustrated, use it as an opportunity to try something new. Maybe it's time to switch up your workout routine, focus on a different area of your fitness, or even take a break and come back with renewed energy. By shifting your perspective, you turn a roadblock into a chance to grow and improve.

Another great way to shift your perspective is to practice gratitude. When you're feeling stuck or discouraged, take a moment to reflect on what's going well. Maybe your progress has slowed, but you're still showing up and putting in the work. Maybe you've faced setbacks, but you've also learned valuable lessons. Gratitude helps you see the bigger picture and reminds you that even in tough times, there's always something to be thankful for.

Turning Obstacles into Opportunities

At the end of the day, obstacles are a natural part of any journey. They're not something to be feared or avoided—they're something to be embraced. Every obstacle you face is an opportunity to learn, grow, and become stronger. It's a chance to prove to yourself that you can overcome challenges and come out on the other side even better than before.

So, the next time you encounter an obstacle, don't let it discourage you. Instead, ask yourself, "What is this trying to teach me? How can I use this to my advantage?" With the right mindset, you can turn any challenge into a stepping stone on your path to success.

Remember, success isn't just about reaching the finish line—it's about the journey you take to get there. And it's often the obstacles you overcome along the way that make the journey so rewarding. So embrace the challenges, learn from your setbacks, and keep moving forward. The road to success is rarely a straight line, but with the right mindset, every twist and turn becomes an opportunity to grow.

Chapter 10: The Power of Community and Connection

As you navigate your fitness and success journey, one of the most valuable assets you can cultivate is a strong sense of community and connection. Surrounding yourself with supportive individuals can elevate your motivation and commitment, making the journey not only more manageable but also a lot more enjoyable. In this chapter, we'll explore the benefits of goal setting with others, finding mentors, engaging in one-on-one accountability walks, and incorporating fun activities like table tennis and 5 miles walk/runs into your routine.

Goal Setting: A Shared Vision

Setting goals is a critical step in any journey, but sharing those goals with others can enhance your commitment and motivation. When you establish goals within a community, you create a shared vision that propels everyone forward. Whether it's friends, coworkers, or a workout group, collaborative goal-setting encourages accountability and fosters a sense of camaraderie.

Consider organizing a monthly meeting with friends or colleagues to discuss your fitness and personal development goals. You can set common objectives, such as running a 5 miles together or completing a fitness challenge, and celebrate your progress as a group. This shared commitment not only keeps you motivated but also builds lasting relationships that make the journey more fulfilling.

Mentoring: Learning from the Best

Finding a mentor can significantly impact your fitness and success journey. A mentor who has already achieved the goals you aspire to can provide invaluable insights and guidance. They can help you navigate challenges, share their experiences, and inspire you to stay focused.

In the fitness realm, a mentor might be an experienced colleague who successfully integrates fitness into their busy life, a personal trainer, or even a member of a local fitness group. Their advice can help you tailor your workouts, overcome obstacles, and stay committed to your goals.

In the workplace, having a mentor can also help you balance your professional ambitions with your fitness goals. They can suggest strategies for time management, introduce you to new fitness resources, or even join you for a workout session. The support and knowledge gained from a mentor can be a game changer, making your journey toward success more informed and efficient.

One-on-One Accountability Walks: Connecting and Moving Forward

One of the simplest yet most effective ways to stay on track with your goals is through one-on-one accountability walks. These walks allow you to combine physical activity with meaningful conversations, creating a supportive environment for sharing progress and setting intentions.

Find a colleague, friend, or mentor who is willing to join you for a weekly walk. Use this time to discuss your fitness objectives, career ambitions, share challenges, and motivate one another. Walking side by side fosters a relaxed atmosphere where ideas and concerns can flow freely. Plus, the physical activity releases endorphins, boosting your mood and helping you feel more energized.

These walks don't have to be lengthy; even a 30-minute stroll can work wonders for both your fitness and mental clarity. Make these accountability walks a regular part of your routine, and you'll find that the combination of movement and connection enhances your journey toward success.

Incorporating Fun Activities: Table Tennis and 5 Mile Walk/Run Events

Fitness doesn't always have to involve intense workouts or long hours at the gym. Introducing fun activities into your routine can make staying active something you look forward to. Activities like table tennis and 5 mile walk/run events are excellent ways to combine fitness with fun, creating a positive atmosphere that encourages participation.

Table Tennis: Setting up a table tennis area in your workplace can provide a quick and enjoyable way to engage in physical activity. Spontaneous matches during breaks not only give you a burst of movement but also foster team spirit and camaraderie. The friendly competition releases endorphins, lifts your spirits, and can even spark creativity in your work.

5 Mile Walk/Run Events: Organizing or participating in local 5 miles walk/run events with colleagues or bosses can be another great way to combine fitness and fun. These events create a sense of community and provide an opportunity for team bonding outside of the office. Training together for the event fosters accountability and allows everyone to share in the excitement of crossing the finish line together.

Participating in these activities as a team enhances the connection between fitness and success, creating a shared experience that strengthens relationships and boosts morale.

The Power of Connection

At the end of the day, the connections you build with others can be one of your most valuable resources on your journey to fitness and success. Whether it's through shared goals, learning from mentors, engaging in accountability walks, or having fun with activities like table tennis and 5 miles events, these connections provide the support and motivation needed to keep you moving forward.

Family Connection

One of the most fulfilling ways to enhance your fitness journey is by exercising with your loved ones—whether that's your spouse, sibling, or child. Working out together not only improves your physical health but also strengthens your emotional bonds. Imagine going for a morning jog with your spouse, where you can catch up on life while boosting your energy for the day ahead. Or think about taking a weekend hike with a sibling, creating shared memories and supporting each other's fitness goals. Even a simple after-dinner walk with your child can turn into a special time for conversation, connection, and mutual encouragement. Exercising with those close to you transforms fitness from a solitary task into a shared experience, making it an enjoyable and meaningful part of your relationship. These moments of togetherness not only contribute to your physical well-being but also enrich your relationships, making the journey toward success a collaborative and rewarding effort.

Remember, you don't have to go it alone. Surround yourself with a community that shares your aspirations and values, and you'll discover that the journey becomes not just easier, but also more rewarding. The

CHAPTER 10: THE POWER OF COMMUNITY AND CONNECTION

power of community and connection can transform your approach to fitness and success, making it a collaborative and enjoyable experience that ultimately leads to greater achievements.

Chapter 11: The Importance of Adaptability

Let's dive into something that might just be one of the most underrated skills on the road to success: adaptability. Life is full of surprises, and no matter how carefully you plan, things rarely go exactly as expected. Whether it's a sudden change in your work situation, a shift in your personal life, or a new challenge in your fitness journey, being able to adapt is crucial. In this chapter, we're going to explore why adaptability matters, how you can develop it, and how it can be a game-changer in your pursuit of success.

Why Adaptability Matters

Here's the thing: change is a challenge though inevitable. No matter how much we might like things to stay the same, the world around us is constantly shifting. New technologies emerge, industries evolve, relationships change, and unexpected events occur. The people who thrive in this ever-changing landscape aren't necessarily the smartest or the strongest—they're the ones who can adapt to new circumstances and make the best of them.

Adaptability isn't just about survival, though; it's also about seizing opportunities. When you're flexible and open to change, you're more likely to spot opportunities that others might miss. You're willing to try new things, take risks, and pivot when necessary. This kind of agility can lead to growth and success in ways that rigidly sticking to a plan never could.

Embracing the Unknown

One of the biggest hurdles to adaptability is the fear of the unknown. Let's face it, change can be scary. When you're used to a certain routine or way of doing things, stepping into the unknown can feel intimidating. But here's the flip side: the unknown is also where growth happens.

Think about it like this: if you never venture outside of your comfort zone, you'll never discover what you're truly capable of. Embracing change, even when it's uncomfortable, opens up new possibilities. It forces you to think creatively, solve problems, and develop new skills.

Instead of viewing change as a threat, try to see it as an adventure. Sure, you might not know exactly what's coming next, but that's part of the excitement. By approaching change with curiosity rather than fear, you can turn uncertainty into a source of motivation rather than stress.

Developing Adaptability

So, how do you become more adaptable? Like any skill, it takes practice. Here are a few strategies to help you develop your adaptability muscles:

Stay Open-Minded: The first step to being adaptable is to keep an open mind. Be willing to consider new ideas, approaches, and perspectives. When faced with a challenge, ask yourself, "Is there another way to look at this?" Staying open-minded helps you see possibilities that you might otherwise overlook.

Embrace Change: Instead of resisting change, make a habit of embracing it. Start with small changes in your daily routine—take a different route to work, try a new hobby, or switch up your workout routine. The more you expose yourself to change, the more comfortable you'll become with it.

Practice Resilience: Adaptability and resilience go hand in hand. When things don't go as planned, resilience helps you bounce back and adapt to new circumstances. To build resilience, focus on maintaining a positive attitude, learning from setbacks, and staying persistent in the face of challenges.

Be Proactive: Don't wait for change to happen—anticipate it. Try to stay informed about trends and developments in your field or area of interest. By staying ahead of the curve, you'll be better prepared to adapt when changes occur.

Learn Continuously: Adaptable people are lifelong learners. They're always looking for ways to improve, grow, and stay relevant. Make a habit of learning new skills, staying curious, and seeking out new experiences. The more you know, the easier it is to adapt to new situations.

Adaptability in Action

Let's look at how adaptability can play out in different areas of life.

In Your Career

In the workplace, adaptability is a highly valued skill. Companies and industries are constantly evolving, and being able to adapt to new technologies, processes, or market conditions can set you apart. For example, during the COVID-19 pandemic, many businesses had to quickly pivot to remote work. Those who were adaptable found ways to thrive in this new environment, while others struggled to adjust.

But it's not just about big changes—being adaptable in your day-to-day work can also lead to success. Maybe a project didn't go as planned, or you've been asked to take on a new role. Instead of seeing these situations as setbacks, view them as opportunities to grow, learn, and showcase your flexibility.

In Your Fitness Journey

When it comes to fitness, adaptability is key to long-term success. Your body changes over time, and so do your goals, preferences, and circumstances. Maybe you've hit a plateau, or perhaps an injury is forcing you to take a break from your usual routine. Instead of getting discouraged, adapt your approach. Try new exercises, explore different types of physical activity, or focus on other aspects of your health, like nutrition or mental wellness.

Being adaptable in your fitness journey also means being willing to adjust your goals as needed. Life happens—whether it's a busy work schedule, family commitments, or a global pandemic, sometimes you need to be flexible with your expectations. Remember, progress isn't always linear, and it's okay to change course if that's what's needed to keep moving forward.

For those periods of life where your routine must be adjusted due to travelling for work or holidays, consider body weight exercises, or resistance weight bands which can be thrown into your suitcase. Small adjustments for a short time, and your body still receives that good feeling of a workout.

In Your Personal Life

Adaptability is just as important in your personal life as it is in your career or fitness journey. Relationships, for instance, require a lot of flexibility. People change, circumstances evolve, and being able to adapt to these changes is crucial for maintaining healthy, happy relationships. Whether it's adapting to a partner's new job, adjusting to parenthood, or navigating a friendship's ups and downs, flexibility helps you grow together rather than apart.

Adaptability also plays a role in managing life's inevitable curveballs. Maybe you've had to move to a new city, deal with a health issue, or navigate a financial challenge. Whatever the situation, being adaptable helps you stay grounded, find solutions, and keep moving forward.

The Payoff of Adaptability

So, what's the payoff for all this adaptability? Simply put, it's the ability to thrive in any situation. When you're adaptable, you're not just surviving change—you're leveraging it to your advantage. You're better equipped to handle whatever life throws at you, and you're more likely to seize opportunities that others might miss.

Adaptability also brings a sense of confidence and peace. When you know that you can handle change, you're less likely to be thrown off course by unexpected events. You become more resilient, more resourceful, and more capable of navigating life's ups and downs.

Financial Investments

Adaptability is crucial not just in navigating life's challenges but also in making informed decisions, especially when it comes to financial investments. Fitness plays a significant role in this process, as a healthy body supports a sharp and resilient mind. Regular exercise enhances

CHAPTER 11: THE IMPORTANCE OF ADAPTABILITY

cognitive function, improves focus, and reduces stress—qualities that are essential when evaluating financial opportunities and risks. When you maintain a disciplined fitness routine, you cultivate a mindset of perseverance and clarity, which can be directly applied to your investment strategies. A strong, adaptable mindset allows you to remain calm under pressure, assess market fluctuations with a clear perspective, and make decisions that are aligned with your long-term financial goals. By prioritizing fitness, you're not just investing in your health but also in the mental acuity needed to fuel smart financial decision-making.

In the end, adaptability is about being open to the journey, wherever it may lead. It's about trusting yourself to find your way, even when the path isn't clear. And it's about recognizing that change, while sometimes uncomfortable, is often the very thing that leads to growth, progress, and ultimately, success.

Chapter 12: Fitness Success with Music (and How It Powers Creativity, Business, and Rest)

Let's talk about one of the best workout partners you can have—music. Whether you're hitting the gym, going for a run, or doing yoga in your living room, the right playlist can take your fitness routine to the next level. But music's influence doesn't stop there. Beyond just helping you power through a workout, music can boost your creativity, help you focus on your studies or business tasks, and even enhance the quality of your rest. In this chapter, we're going to explore how music can be a driving force in not just your fitness success, but in your overall success as well.

The Science Behind Music and Exercise

Ever wonder why your favorite song can instantly make you feel more energized? There's solid science behind the connection between music and exercise. When you listen to music, especially something with a strong beat, it triggers the release of dopamine—a feel-good chemical in your brain. This boost of dopamine can improve your mood, increase your motivation, and make your workout feel more enjoyable.

But that's not all. Music can also help you stay in sync with your movements, making your exercise feel more rhythmic and natural. Think about it—when you're running or lifting weights to the beat of a song, you're more likely to keep a steady pace and maintain good form. This rhythm can help you push through the tough parts of your workout, especially when you're starting to feel tired.

And let's not forget about music's ability to distract you from discomfort. When you're focused on the lyrics or the melody, you're less likely to notice how hard you're working. This means you might be able to go longer or push harder without even realizing it. It's like a mental trick that helps you get the most out of your workout.

Choosing the Right Music for Your Workout

Not all music is created equal when it comes to working out. The key is to find songs that match the intensity and type of exercise you're doing. Here's a breakdown of how to choose the right music for different types of workouts:

High-Intensity Workouts:

For activities like running, cycling, or HIIT (High-Intensity Interval Training), you'll want music with a fast tempo and a strong beat. Songs with 120 to 140 beats per minute (BPM) are ideal for these kinds of workouts. Think upbeat pop, rock, or electronic music that gets your heart pumping and keeps you motivated to push through.

Strength Training:

When you're lifting weights, you might want something a little slower but still powerful. Songs with a strong, steady beat can help you stay focused on your reps and maintain good form. Look for music in the 90 to 120 BPM range, like hip-hop or slower rock tunes that have a strong rhythm.

Cardio:

For steady-state cardio like a long run, brisk walk, or cycling session, you'll want music that helps you keep a consistent pace. Mid-tempo songs around 120 BPM are perfect for keeping you moving without burning out too quickly. Pop, dance, or even some upbeat R&B can work well here.

Yoga or Stretching:

When it comes to yoga, stretching, or cool-downs, you'll want music that's calming and soothing. Look for slower songs with a tempo of 60 to 90 BPM, like ambient music, acoustic tracks, or mellow indie tunes. The goal here is to help you relax and focus on your breathing and movement.

Interval Training:

If you're doing intervals, where you alternate between periods of high intensity and rest, consider using a playlist that mimics this pattern. Choose a mix of fast-paced songs for your high-intensity intervals and slower songs for your recovery periods. This way, the music guides you through the workout and keeps you on track.

Music as a Creative Force

While music is great for your body, it's also a powerful tool for your mind, especially when it comes to creativity. Whether you're brainstorming new ideas for a business project, working on a creative hobby, or studying for an exam, music can help unlock your creative potential and keep you focused.

Boosting Creativity:

Music can serve as a catalyst for creativity. Listening to music that inspires you can help you think outside the box and come up with innovative ideas. For creative tasks, instrumental music, ambient sounds, or even classical tunes can help set the mood without distracting you with lyrics. Some people find that listening to music they're already familiar with helps them focus, as it fades into the background and lets their mind wander freely.

Enhancing Focus and Productivity:

When you're working on a business project or studying, music can help create an environment that fosters concentration. The right background music can block out distractions and help you maintain a steady workflow. Again, instrumental music is often best for these situations, as it allows you to focus on the task at hand without the interference of lyrics. Genres like lo-fi hip-hop, ambient electronic music, or even nature sounds are popular choices for enhancing productivity.

Setting the Tone for Business Success:

Music isn't just for individual tasks—it can also set the tone for your entire work environment. In an office setting, playing upbeat, positive music can create a motivating atmosphere that boosts morale and productivity. On the other hand, when you need to focus deeply, switching to calming, unobtrusive music can help you and your team concentrate better.

The Role of Music in Rest and Recovery

We've talked a lot about how music can energize and motivate you, but it's just as important to recognize its role in rest and recovery. Whether you're winding down after a tough workout, taking a power nap, or trying to get a good night's sleep, the right music can help you relax and recharge.

Enhancing Power Naps:

Power naps are a fantastic way to recharge during a busy day, and music can make them even more effective. Soft, calming music or even binaural beats can help you relax quickly, allowing you to drift off into a restful nap. The right music can create a peaceful environment that blocks out distracting noises and helps you wake up feeling refreshed.

Promoting Quality Sleep:

Just as music can help you power through a workout, it can also help you unwind at the end of the day. Listening to calming music before bed can signal to your body that it's time to relax and prepare for sleep. Studies have shown that listening to music with a slow tempo can help lower your heart rate and breathing, making it easier to fall asleep and stay asleep. Consider creating a bedtime playlist with soft, soothing songs to help you drift off peacefully.

Aid in Meditation and Mindfulness:

Music is a great companion for meditation and mindfulness practices, which are essential for mental and emotional recovery. Whether you're practicing deep breathing, guided meditation, or simply taking a few minutes to sit quietly, soft music can help set the mood and keep you centered.

Creating Your Ultimate Playlist for Success

Now that you know how music can boost your fitness, creativity, productivity, and rest, it's time to create the ultimate playlist that supports all areas of your life. Here's how to do it:

Segment Your Playlist:

Consider creating different segments or even multiple playlists for different activities. You might have one playlist for high-intensity workouts, another for creative work, and yet another for winding down. This way, you can easily switch to the right music depending on what you're doing.

Include a Mix of Genres:

Just as variety is important in your workout playlist, it's also key in a playlist designed for overall success. Include a mix of genres and styles to keep things interesting and to suit different moods and activities. For example, you might include upbeat pop for exercise, classical music for focus, and ambient tunes for relaxation.

Update Regularly:

Keep your playlist fresh by regularly adding new songs and removing ones you've overplayed. This helps keep your workouts, work sessions, and rest times exciting and gives you something to look forward to each time.

Use Music as a Reward:

Sometimes, the best motivation is knowing that you'll get to listen to your favorite tunes. Use music as a reward for completing a tough workout, finishing a big project, or even just getting through a challenging day. This can make your music experience feel even more special and rewarding.

The Emotional and Mental Benefits of Music

Beyond the practical benefits, music can also provide an emotional and mental boost that enhances your overall well-being. Certain songs have the power to evoke memories, stir emotions, or make you feel inspired. Tapping into this emotional power can make your workouts more enjoyable, your creative work more fulfilling, and your rest more restorative.

For example, you might include songs that remind you of a special moment in your life or that make you feel empowered. These tracks can give you that extra push when you need it most, helping you tap into a deeper level of motivation and inspiration.

Sing a Song

Music has an incredible power to influence our mood, energy levels, and even our success. Whether you're powering through a workout or visualising a project idea, the right playlist can make all the difference. But it's not just about the beats you listen to in the gym—something as simple as singing along to your favorite songs in the car can have a profound impact on your mindset. When you belt out those tunes during your commute, you're not just passing the time; you're boosting your confidence and releasing dopamine, the feel-good chemical that enhances happiness. This surge of positivity can spill over into other areas of your life, creating a success loop where you feel more motivated, creative, and ready to tackle whatever challenges come your way. So next time you're driving, don't hesitate to turn up the volume and sing your heart out—it's not just fun; it's a powerful tool for fueling your success.

Final Thoughts: Let the Music Guide Your Success

At the end of the day, music is a powerful tool that can elevate every aspect of your life. It can boost your mood, enhance your performance, and make your workouts, work, and rest more enjoyable. Whether you're running a marathon, brainstorming a new business idea, or just trying to relax after a long day, the right music can be the difference between good and great.

So, next time you're gearing up for a workout, tackling a big project, or preparing for a well-deserved rest, take a few minutes to put together a playlist that gets you pumped and ready to succeed. Let the music be your guide, your motivator, and your companion as you work toward your goals. And remember, it's not just about the physical benefits—music can make your journey more fun, more inspiring, and ultimately, more successful in every way.

Conclusion: Fit for the Top

As we've journeyed through this book, one thing has become crystal clear: fitness is not just about looking good or hitting a certain number on the scale. It's about building the physical, mental, and emotional strength you need to succeed in every area of your life. Whether you're striving to climb the corporate ladder, launch your own business, or simply live a happier, healthier life, fitness is the foundation that supports all of these goals.

Recapping the Importance of Fitness in Achieving and Sustaining Success

We've covered a lot of ground, from the basics of building a fitness routine that works for you to the more nuanced ways that physical health impacts your mental clarity, emotional resilience, and overall productivity. Let's recap some of the key points:

Fitness Fuels Productivity: A strong body leads to a strong mind. Regular exercise boosts your energy levels, sharpens your focus, and enhances your ability to tackle challenges with confidence. When you prioritize your fitness, you're also prioritizing your ability to perform at your best in your work and personal life.

Resilience Through Routine: A consistent fitness routine teaches discipline, perseverance, and the ability to push through discomfort. These qualities are essential not just in the gym, but in the boardroom, the classroom, and every other aspect of life where success is the goal.

Mental Clarity and Emotional Balance: Exercise isn't just good for your body; it's also crucial for your mental and emotional health. Regular physical activity reduces stress, improves mood, and fosters a sense of well-being—all of which are key ingredients for sustainable success.

The Power of Habits: Success in fitness and in life is built on the habits you cultivate. By establishing a regular workout routine, you're laying the groundwork for other positive habits that can lead to success in your career, relationships, and beyond.

The Role of Recovery: Just as important as the effort you put in is the recovery time you allow yourself. Rest, relaxation, and proper nutrition are vital components of any fitness plan and are equally important in maintaining balance and preventing burnout in your professional and personal life.

The Journey Ahead: Maintaining Momentum in Fitness and Life

As you move forward, the key to sustaining your success is to keep the momentum going. Fitness is not a one-time achievement; it's a lifelong journey. The same goes for success in your career, studies, or any other personal goals. It's all about building momentum and maintaining it over time.

Set New Goals: Don't stop at the goals you've already achieved. Continuously set new, challenging goals for yourself in both fitness and life. This will keep you motivated, prevent stagnation, and ensure that you're always moving forward.

Stay Flexible: Life is unpredictable, and there will be times when your routine is disrupted. The key is to stay flexible and adapt. If you miss a workout or fall off track with your goals, don't dwell on it. Adjust your plan and get back on course.

Celebrate Progress: Take time to celebrate your achievements, no matter how small. Acknowledging your progress keeps you motivated and reminds you of how far you've come.

Keep Learning: Fitness and success are both about continuous improvement. Stay curious, keep learning, and be open to new strategies, techniques, and ideas that can help you on your journey.

Final Thoughts on the Fitness-Success Journey

Your fitness journey is more than just a quest for physical strength or endurance; it's a path that runs parallel to your journey toward success in every aspect of life. By committing to your health, you're making an investment in your future—a future where you have the energy, resilience, and confidence to tackle whatever challenges come your way.

Remember, success is not just about reaching the top—it's about staying there, maintaining your momentum, and continuing to grow. Fitness provides the foundation, the strength, and the discipline needed to not only achieve your goals but to sustain your success over the long term.

So, as you step into the next phase of your journey, carry these lessons with you. Embrace the power of fitness as a tool for success, and let it guide you to new heights. Stay fit, stay focused, and stay unstoppable. The top is within your reach—and with the right mindset and habits, you'll not only get there, but you'll thrive.

Appendix

This appendix is designed to provide you with practical resources to support your fitness journey and success. Whether you're a busy professional trying to squeeze in a workout, looking for nutritional advice to boost your performance, or eager to dive deeper into the connection between fitness and success, this section has you covered.

Recommended Fitness Programs for Busy Professionals

Finding time to exercise can be challenging, especially with a packed schedule. Here are some efficient, effective programs tailored for busy professionals:

HIIT (High-Intensity Interval Training):

Duration: 20–30 minutes

Frequency: 3–4 times per week

Overview: HIIT workouts involve short bursts of intense exercise followed by brief recovery periods. They're highly effective for burning calories, improving cardiovascular health, and building strength—all in a fraction of the time compared to traditional workouts.

Suggested Programs:

Seven-Minute Workout App: A quick, equipment-free routine that targets all major muscle groups.

FitOn: Offers a variety of HIIT workouts ranging from beginner to advanced levels.

Strength Training:

Duration: 30–45 minutes

Frequency: 3 times per week

Overview: Strength training builds muscle, boosts metabolism, and enhances overall body composition. Focus on compound exercises like squats, deadlifts, and bench presses for maximum efficiency.

Suggested Programs:

StrongLifts 5x5: A straightforward program that focuses on five core lifts to build strength.

BodyBoss Ultimate Body Guide: Combines strength training with HIIT for a well-rounded workout.

Yoga and Stretching:

Duration: 15–30 minutes

Frequency: Daily or as needed

Overview: Yoga and stretching improve flexibility, reduce stress, and promote mindfulness—perfect for counteracting the effects of a sedentary job.

Suggested Programs:

Yoga with Adriene: Free YouTube videos ranging from quick 10-minute sessions to full-length classes.

Daily Yoga App: Offers a wide range of yoga routines tailored to your fitness level and goals.

Quick Cardio Routines:

Duration: 20–30 minutes

Frequency: 4–5 times per week

Overview: Short, intense cardio sessions are ideal for boosting energy levels, improving heart health, and burning calories in a limited amount of time.

Suggested Programs:

Couch to 5 miles: A beginner-friendly running program that gradually increases your endurance.

Peloton Digital: Provides a variety of quick cardio workouts, including cycling, running, and dance.

Nutritional Guides for Enhanced Performance

Nutrition is a key component of your fitness and success journey. Here are some guidelines and resources to help you fuel your body for peak performance:

Balanced Diet for Busy Professionals:

Focus on: Whole foods, lean proteins, healthy fats, and complex carbohydrates.

Quick Tips:

Meal Prep: Prepare meals in advance to avoid unhealthy food choices when time is tight.

Hydration: Aim for at least 8 glasses of water a day to stay hydrated and energized.

Snack Smart: Keep healthy snacks like nuts, fruits, and yogurt on hand to maintain energy levels throughout the day.

Performance-Enhancing Nutrition:

Protein: Essential for muscle repair and growth. Include lean meats, fish, eggs, and plant-based proteins like beans and tofu in your diet.

Carbohydrates: Your body's primary energy source. Opt for whole grains, fruits, and vegetables to fuel your workouts.

Fats: Healthy fats from sources like avocados, nuts, and olive oil support brain function and hormone production.

Supplements: Consider adding a multivitamin, omega-3 fatty acids, and vitamin D to your regimen if you have dietary gaps. Consult with a healthcare provider before starting any supplements.

Recommended Resources:

Precision Nutrition: Offers personalized nutrition coaching and educational resources for optimizing diet and performance.

MyFitnessPal: A user-friendly app that helps track your food intake, set nutrition goals, and stay on top of your diet.

Resources for Further Reading on Fitness and Success

If you're interested in delving deeper into the connection between fitness and success, these books, articles, and websites offer valuable insights and inspiration:

Books:

"Spark: The Revolutionary New Science of Exercise and the Brain" by John J. Ratey: Explores how exercise improves brain function, enhances mood, and boosts performance.

"The Power of Habit: Why We Do What We Do in Life and Business" by Charles Duhigg: Understand how habits are formed and how to create positive routines that support your fitness and success goals.

"Atomic Habits: An Easy & Proven Way to Build Good Habits & Break Bad Ones" by James Clear: A practical guide to making small changes that lead to big results in both fitness and life.

Articles:

"How Exercise Shapes You, Far Beyond the Gym" (by Brad Stulberg): Discusses the broader impacts of fitness on leadership, productivity, and overall success.

"The Exercise Effect: Evidence on How Fitness Boosts Your Mental and Emotional Health" (American Psychological Association): A comprehensive overview of the psychological benefits of regular physical activity.

Resources

Harmon, M. (2024, July 16). The 10 best workout and fitness apps of 2024. Forbes Health. https://www.forbes.com/health/fitness/best-fitness-apps/

Garone, S. (2023, May 31). Get Mo' Mojo: 10 tips to boost your workout motivation. Greatist. https://greatist.com/fitness/workout-motivation

How exercise can boost success at work. (n.d.). The Body Coach. https://www.thebodycoach.com/blog/how-exercise-can-boost-success-at-work/#:~:text=Exercise%20can%20boost%20concentration%2C%20help,on%20all%20cylinders%20at%20work.&text=Another%20reason%20successful%20people%20keep,more%20energy%20in%20the%20workplace.

The 7 minute workout app - seven. (n.d.). Seven. https://seven.app/

FitOn. (n.d.). Fitness Routines - FitOn. FitOn - #1 Free Fitness App, Stop Paying for Home Workouts. https://fitonapp.com/fitness/

Stronglifts 5×5 workout program: Quick Start Guide | Stronglifts. (2024, March 4). Stronglifts. https://stronglifts.com/stronglifts-5x5/workou

t-program/

The BodyBoss method. (n.d.). BodyBoss. https://au.bodyboss.com/pages/method

Yoga With Adriene, LLC. (2024, August 5). Yoga with Adriene. Yoga With Adriene. https://yogawithadriene.com/

Personalized Chair Yoga Plan. (n.d.). https://www.dailyyoga.com/

Couch to 5 miles - C25 miles Running Program. (2024, May 2). Couch to 5 miles - C25 miles running program. Couch to 5 miles - C25 miles Running Program | C25 miles Has Been Designed to Get Just About Anyone From the Couch to Running 5 Kilometers or 30 Minutes in Just 9 Weeks. https://c25 miles.com/

Peloton: The ultimate fitness experience. (n.d.). https://www.onepeloton.com/

Precision Nutrition. (2024, August 15). Nutrition Certification, coaching & Courses | Precision Nutrition. https://www.precisionnutrition.com/

Calorie Tracker & BMR calculator to reach your goals | MyFitnessPal. (n.d.). https://www.myfitnesspal.com/

VanBergeijk, E. (2014). John J. Ratey (2008): Spark: The revolutionary new science of exercise and the brain. Unabridged, 9 hours, 28 minutes. Journal of Autism and Developmental Disorders, 44(4), 990–991. https://doi.org/10.1007/s10803-014-2044-7

James, S. E. (2012). Charles Duhigg: The Power of Habit: Why we do what we do in life and business. Journal of Child and Family Studies, 22(4),

582–584. https://doi.org/10.1007/s10826-012-9645-6

Wikipedia contributors. (2023, December 9). The Power of Habit. Wikipedia. https://en.wikipedia.org/wiki/The_Power_of_Habit

Stulberg, B. (2018, June 11). How exercise shapes you, far beyond the gym - personal growth - medium. Medium. https://medium.com/personal-growth/how-exercise-shapes-you-far-beyond-the-gym

Weir, K. (n.d.). The exercise effect. https://www.apa.org. https://www.apa.org/monitor/2011/12/exercise

Final Thoughts

By incorporating the recommended fitness programs, nutritional guides, and further reading resources into your routine, you'll be well-equipped to maintain your fitness and success journey. Remember, the pursuit of success is ongoing, and staying fit—both physically and mentally—is crucial for achieving and sustaining it. Keep pushing forward, stay curious, and never stop learning. The journey is as important as the destination.

If you found this book helpful, I'd be very appreciative if you left an honest favorable review and star rating for this book on Amazon or wherever you bought this book.

Cheers to your success.

www.ingramcontent.com/pod-product-compliance
Lightning Source LLC
Chambersburg PA
CBHW051534240526
45471CB00020B/2672